DOGS AND PEOPLE

Dogs and People

GORDON CARTER

illustrated with photographs

ABELARD - SCHUMAN

London   New York   Toronto

by the same author:
Dogs at Work
Willing Walkers

© Gordon Carter 1968
First published 1968
First published in U.S.A. 1969
L.C.C.C. Number 69-11047
Standard Book Number 200.71520.8

LONDON
Abelard-Schuman
Limited
8 King Street WC2

NEW YORK
Abelard-Schuman
Limited
6 West 57 Street

TORONTO
Abelard-Schuman
Canada Limited
Scarborough Ontario

Acknowledgements

The preparation of this book and the permission to reproduce photographs could not have been attempted without the kind assistance of many individuals and organizations. Grateful acknowledgements are paid to all concerned, and especially to the following:—

American Humane Association, Denver, Colorado, U.S.A.
American Kennel Club, New York, U.S.A.
The American Society for the Prevention of Cruelty to Animals, New York, U.S.A.
American Veterinary Medical Associations, Chicago, Illinois, U.S.A.
Boston Terrier Club of America.
Dog's Home, Battersea, London.
Gaines Dog Research Centre, New York, U.S.A.
Kennel Club, London
Ralston Purina Company, St. Louis, Missouri, U.S.A.
Royal Society for the Prevention of Cruelty to Animals, London.
Royal Society for the Prevention of Cruelty to Animals, Liverpool Branch.
People's Dispensary for Sick Animals, Dorking, Surrey.

Contents

Illustrations

Introduction

This is the book I have always wanted to write about dogs. However, interesting as it may be to read about a certain breed or about a particular type of dog, there is nothing quite so fascinating as an account of the things dogs and humans do together. This is what *Dogs and People* is about. There were some difficulties involved in telling this story. There was not enough room to mention all the large number of breeds, nor all the people who played a part in the history of this man-dog relationship. But most of the breeds which are well known in Great Britain and the United States are included, as well as the principal people who have played an important part in the changing fortunes of the canine world.

Dogs and People describes events which have helped to shape the relationships between dogs and their human masters through the ages. Dogs and people did not always live as happily together as they do now. Certain people managed to improve the conditions under which dogs lived and to change people's attitudes towards them. This book brings to attention the remarkable and fairly recent concern that many people now have for the health and treatment of dogs and some of the miracles of surgery performed on them. You will also read of ways in which people and dogs have risked their lives for each other. There are some interesting stories, too, of famous men and women and their dogs at the end of the book.

I do hope that all my readers will enjoy the chapters following this introduction, and that some of the photographs will remind them of their own pets. I repeat that I am sorry that every breed is not included. But I do hope that when you have finished reading, you will understand why I wanted to write this book.

1 : Early Dogs

Nowadays, no other animal enjoys the same close friendship with their owners as a dog. But this relationship took a long time to develop, and is far from the ways things began. Dogs, which lived thousands of years before Christ, did not look at all like the pets of today. You would not have known the difference between foxes, jackals, wolves and wild dogs. For then, all dogs were wild animals.

The remains of a genuine dog of about 2,000 B.C., were discovered during an excavation at Windmill Hill, in Wiltshire, England, just before the outbreak of the Second World War. This dog did not have the features of any particular breed. Nor is it likely to have been used for any special task. It was probably semi-wild, spending most of its time with a pack, but wintering with a human being. In bad weather shelter and scraps of food were more important to it than any loyalty to its own kind.

We can only guess at the way man treated his fickle canine visitor. He is not likely to have made a pet of it. To him it was just another animal in a world of wild creatures and human enemies. Even so, its noisy barking would have made it a useful guard against surprise attacks. Its senses would have been much keener than today's domesticated dog. He quite likely sometimes took it on hunting expeditions. But it would have been too unreliable to be used in those which were really dangerous or important.

During the Bronze Age, as man kept some domesticated animals, dogs were probably kept, too. Later, during the Iron Age, excavations revealed that two types of dog were common. Both were bigger than the dog found in Wiltshire. One was a dog of medium build, thickset and powerful, similar to chows and other huskies. It had a long narrow muzzle and a broad flat head. The other, which was larger, was probably a mastiff, a less common breed.

The medium sized dog may have been a descendant of the Wiltshire discovery, mentioned earlier. The mastiff was most likely brought from across the seas by marauding invaders such as the Halstatt Celts. These fierce warriors were renowned for their battle dogs. Their huge dogs must have terrified their enemies.

Dogs were also being used by peoples in countries other than England. The ancient Egyptians were aware of dogs' usefulness in hunting and in battle. They had a great respect for good hunters and courageous warriors. They also kept dogs in their homes as pets and children loved to play with toy dogs.

The mastiff was one of the earliest types of dogs used by man.

Photo: *Studio Lisa Ltd.*

The Babylonians bred and kept dogs although they did not use them as much as the Egyptians. Some old carvings show mastiffs chained to their owners. As you can imagine, these large dogs made good bodyguards against attack by robbers and other criminals. Wealthy people were always fair game, and were likely to be set upon by thieves whenever they went out by themselves. So, in many early civilizations, dogs were usually associated with rich people. They were also allowed to roam loose to frighten off beggars, lunatics and lepers.

The Bible gives a vivid picture of how much the ordinary people hated dogs. When they are mentioned at all, it is with disgust, loathing and contempt. But it must be remembered that dogs could be dangerous as carriers of disease in hot climates. They also ravaged flocks and herds, and were the same sort of menace to the Israelites that foxes and wolves are to many farmers today.

There are bitter references to dogs in the psalms. One of David's psalms includes a heart-rending passage when God is accused of neglecting him. "My God, my God, look upon me. Why have you forsaken me! . . . Many bulls have compassed me . . . Dogs, too, have pressed in on me. . . Deliver my soul from the sword and my dearest from the power of the dog."

The Assyrians, who lived in what is now Iraq, are known to have had dogs. They were not really kept for sentimental reasons as the Assyrians' attitude was to treat dogs as faithful and hardworking animals essential for certain outdoor pursuits. As far back as the century before Christ, the

Assyrian royal household kept large kennels of mastiffs and salukis for their field sport, and took a large number of dogs with them on these expeditions. It needed great wealth to feed and maintain such formidable hunting packs.

Across the Mediterranean in Europe, dogs had a place in the mighty civilizations of Greece and Rome. But the ancient Greeks had little affection for them. However, there was so much general ill-treatment of and ignorance about all animals, at that period, and for long afterwards, that even the absence of harshness and cruelty was proof of a certain acceptance.

Although the Greeks used dogs for hunting, and for guarding their homes and flocks, they did not realize their great qualities. There is little written about dogs in Greek literature. The epic poet, Homer, uses the word "dog" to describe a cowardly person. From this we can guess that the skulking presence of wild dogs as scavengers was as common in the southeastern parts of Europe as in the eastern countries.

One of the few writers to mention dogs was the famous Greek general, Xenophon. The General's chief interest in dogs was connected with hunting. This is how he described the the hounds he liked to use. "In the first place they should be big; and in the second place they should have light, flat, well-knit heads. The lower part of the face should be sinewy and the eyes black, bright and prominent; the face large and broad, with a deep space between the eyes; ears long, thin and bare on the outside; neck long, soft and flexible; breast broad and fleshy. . . ."

Xenophon went on to give an account of how hounds

hunted. "In hunting, they ought to learn to quit the beaten tracks, slanting their heads towards the ground, smelling. When they are actually near the hare, then they should give the sign to the huntsman, by running about much more quickly than before, signifying by their eagerness, and with the head, the eye and their entire change of carriage, by their looking towards or at the hare's hiding place, and moving their bodies forwards, backwards and sideways, by their obvious joy and delight, that they are near the hare."

Xenophon emphasized that the hounds should not return to the huntsman once the hare is spotted. And it was not enough that they looked right and were adaptable. Hounds used for hunting should be faster than the average dog and had to be "of the superior kind" in spirit. He also held a view that is still held in many hunting circles and by dog authorities. He believed that hounds of one colour were not wellbred. Xenophon preferred a dog to be of three colours. And many of today's dog fanciers still believe that dogs of mixed colours are better than those of only one colour.

The Romans were aware of how useful dogs could be as guards and hunters as well as warriors and entertainers in the arenas. They had great respect for the faithful guard and brave hunter. Cicero writes of them, "Such fidelity of dogs in protecting what is committed to their charge, such affectionate attachment to their masters, such suspicion of strangers, such extraordinary scenting ability in following a track, such concentration in hunting – what else do they prove than the creation of these animals for the use of man?"

Another writer, Marcus Varro, who was experienced in the breeding and raising of puppies, gave the following advice about dogs: "There are two kinds, one for hunting connected with the wild beasts of the woods, the other, trained for defence of flocks and herds and used by shepherds. . . . Be careful to avoid buying dogs from hunters and butchers; the latter are too idle to follow, while hunting dogs are too easily distracted by hares and will leave the sheep to chase them." Varro recommended people to buy dogs which had been trained, when young, by shepherds.

But there was a great surprise in store for the Romans who invaded Britain in 55 B.C. They were amazed at the size of the mastiffs used by the fierce islanders in battle against them. Caesar's disciplined legions did not much relish taking on these huge animals. They were superior by far to the large fighting dogs used in the Roman arenas. But as soon as they had conquered the islanders, they lost no time in sending some mastiffs back to their friends and families at home. It was not long before these powerful dogs were among the most formidable to be found in the Roman arenas.

It is not until some time after the decline of the Roman Empire that we can find much written about dogs and the way they were treated. Some laws were passed during the reigns of early British monarchs.

During the time of Alfred the Great (849–901), dog owners were heavily fined if their animals attacked people. The fines had to be paid even if the dog escaped.

About a century later, laws made by King Edgar refer to

Top: Hunters with nets and mastiffs
Bottom: Mastiffs being used with horses
From a wall frieze in the palace of Ashurbanipal, a famous Assyrian king
of the Bronze Age period.

Photo: *British Museum*

dog collars which were called "informed" if they carried a bell. They were made of leather, were wide and had nails or pointed studs fastened to their outside, to protect the dog's neck from attack, especially when hunting.

Howell the Good, Prince of Wales, listed the known dogs in his country as the buckhound, the colwyn (probably a kind of spaniel), the greyhound, the tracker, watchdog, shepherd dog and peasant dog. A trained dog was valued at a pound, the others were worth ten shillings. However, the poor dog used by a peasant only cost fourpence.

There were no restrictions on poaching then, and Welsh and Saxons roamed the great forests with their dogs to their hearts' content. There was plenty of game to keep the dogs and their masters busy among the wild stretches of trees.

Later, Danish kings introduced laws to discourage poaching. These were severe enough to put most people off. Death was the penalty for those caught hunting on crown lands.

The practical use of the dog by the early British was in sharp contrast with the customs of the Parsees in India. Kindness to animals was an important principle of their faith, and dogs held a high position. They had to be correctly fed and looked after. Their standards were high for they were a very clean and tidy people. It was considered a crime to neglect and ill-treat animals, especially dogs.

The following extract, taken from the sacred book of the Parsees, shows how they regarded a dog's character.

"He eats broken food like a priest; he is grateful, like a

priest; he is easily satisfied, like a priest; he wants only a small piece of bread, like a priest. He marches in front, like a warrior; he fights for the beneficent cows, like a warrior; he goes first out of the house, like a warrior. He is watchful and sleeps lightly, like a husbandman; he goes first out of the house, like a husbandman; he returns last into the house, like a husbandman. . . .

The Chinese and Japanese also held dogs in high esteem. Interest in dogs was particularly keen in China. Dog watching was something of a hobby, rather like bird watching is nowadays. Dogs were observed closely, and their habits noted and jotted down. New or unusual breeds drew excited attention. There were many kennel masters, and some dog trainers. There is no doubt that China was a nation of enthusiastic dog lovers.

Marco Polo, the famous Venetian traveller, was one of the first Europeans to visit China. He arrived there in 1275 and stayed for seventeen years. When he returned to Venice, his stories of what he had seen and heard seemed almost incredible to the people of his own country.

His book of travels contained much information about dogs, mostly true although exaggerated in parts. One typical story tells of two brothers employed by a prince as Keepers of the Mastiffs. "Each of them has 10,000 men and 5,000 dogs under his control—they move along well, all in line, so that the whole length extends over a whole day's journey, and no animal can escape them. It is a glorious sight to see the working of the dogs and huntsmen at such times. And as the prince himself rides a-fowling across the plains, the big hounds come rushing up, one pack after a bear, another after a deer. . . . It is a wonderful sport and spectacle."

Marco Polo was very impressed by the mastiffs which he called "those big dogs" or "those big hounds" according to the way they were used. He described vividly the way they drew sleds across the winter snows. "On such a sledge, they lay a bearskin on which the courier sits, and the sledge is drawn by six of those big dogs that I spoke of. The dogs have no driver but go straight for the next posthouse, drawing the sledge easily over the ice and snow."

If this were really true, then the Chinese must have been extraordinarily advanced in training dogs. But most likely Marco Polo was exaggerating somewhat. Dog teams do not work well together unless they have a human driver, however good or well-trained their canine leader is. Marco Polo then goes on to describe how the sled is drawn as far as a relay station where fresh dogs, pulling another sled, take over. The others return slowly to the place where they started from.

Half a century later, an Englishman, called Robert Fortune, wrote about the dogs he saw in China: "I had never seen Chinese dogs hunting before, and was highly amused with their performance. They seem to have little or no scent, but they do possess a quick eye, and swift foot, and a wounded animal rarely gets away from them.

Fortune also visited Japan, where he saw some toy dogs. "The lap dogs of the country are highly prized both by natives and foreigners. They are small—some of them not more than ten inches in length. They are remarkable for snub noses and sunken eyes, and are certainly more curious than beautiful."

This description is too similar to the Pekingese to be a coincidence. This breed of toy dog which was thought to have originated in China, came from Japan. The Chinese imported it into China some time during the first century A.D.

In contrast, the treatment of dogs in the West was generally harsh. The Normans, who settled in Britain after the invasion of 1066, adored hunting and tightened the laws against poaching on their estates. No large dogs were allowed to roam in the forests. Except for sheep dogs, medium-sized dogs were not allowed either, unless they could pass through a measuring ring. This was usually so small that not many dogs could get through it. If a man or his dog were caught chasing game, the fine was so heavy that the man was financially crippled for years. A dog might be maimed, if he were considered dangerous to game.

Even so, poaching persisted. Many men were fond of hunting and it provided them with a source of meat. Forests were too big to be properly patrolled, and many highwaymen and outlaws sought refuge in their leafy shelter.

Few wealthy people travelled without a mastiff or two to protect them. The poorer people, who lived on the edge of woods and forests, used dogs for poaching and warning off strangers.

So, in spite of restrictions and harsh punishments, poaching

The earliest Pekingese dogs originated in Japan.

Photo: *Purina Pet Foods*

with dogs continued. King John, 1199–1216, was so determined to stop poaching on his estates that he ordered any dogs found trespassing to be destroyed. He believed this was a more effective way to stop poaching than taking measures against their masters.

So, whether as a guard or hunter the dog had no rights. Its death was mourned only as the loss of a piece of useful property. Dogs were not considered important as living creatures in their own right. Many centuries were to pass before they were to be looked upon as companions.

2 : Hunting, Shooting, Swimming and Racing

The names of many dogs have links with times when life was very different from our own. Some of today's pets come from a hardworking past, stretching back long before the Roman Empire, when hunting was the popular pastime. Dogs had a serious job to do and were rarely looked upon as companions, except in parts of Italy and the Netherlands. Even books which appeared in the fifteenth century, if they mentioned dogs at all, were concerned only with their usefulness.

A curious poem appeared in the *Book of St. Albans*, published in 1486. It was about a greyhound and was probably intended for children to learn by heart. No doubt, they found its rules valuable later when they went hunting. It emphasized what they should look for.

> The greyhound should be headed like a snake,
> And necked like a drake,
> Footed like a cat,

Tailed like a rat,
Ribbed like a beam,
Glossy like a bream,
The first year he should learn to feed,
The second learn to follow on a lead.

Another book. *The History of Four Footed Beasts*, by Topsell, 1607, also gave an interesting slant on dogs. After a fascinating description of water dogs, which referred to water spaniels or poodles, the author warned his readers against clipping them.

"In a really hot summer, there may be some excuse for doing this, but surely not at other times. Nature provides the dog with the equipment it needs and the coat of the water dog protects it against the icy effects of water. Take away any part of the coat by shaving and the dog will not be too keen to swim. If the hair is matted and hard it is, of course, true that this weight will drag in water and reduce speed—all that needs to be done is a thorough combing. But shaving off a dog's hair, if continued, will only discourage it from work and it will eventually lose interest. Any ordinary land spaniel, unused to water, will tire any twenty overshaven dogs in water."

Hounds have been bred and used for hunting a wide variety of animals. They have trailed and chased deer, boars, hares, foxes, badgers, otters, raccoons, wolves and even lions.

Two groups of dogs, many of which are now admired as pets, were formerly only used for hunting. One group, made up of medium-sized and large breeds like hounds, pointers, setters and spaniels, were employed above ground. The other group consisted mainly of smaller dogs—terriers (from the Latin word *terra*, meaning earth or ground)—which would go down into holes, squeeze between crevices, or even burrow below ground to find their prey.

The fast moving dogs, like greyhounds, hunt by sight, while the stronger but bulkier and more cumbersome dogs track by scent, and lead their masters to the quarry. In areas heavily forested or overgrown, small hounds are held by leashes. They ferret out animals which have been tracked down but have hidden themselves in the undergrowth. Large hounds, like the French Talbot, lighter and darker than blood hounds, were often used for hunting deer, but were at a disadvantage where smaller and faster animals were concerned.

In Central Europe, deer was one of the most popular animals to be hunted, and boar hunting was also a much-liked sport. The British chased the hare, or anything that gave them an excuse to hunt. The country squire and the wealthier farmer always had a few dogs around and would go out with them at any time of the day, if there were the prospect of a good chase. Some villages kept their own pack of hounds.

But it was rather a haphazard affair, and it was not until the beginning of the eighteenth century that certain types of hounds were set aside for special kinds of hunting.

In Sussex and the south of England, a large and rather plodding type of hare-hunting hound was used, known as the Southern hound. In France, a smaller edition of this breed was called the basset hound, now a very popular dog in Britain and the United States.

But the modern basset is a result of breeding the original animals with the bloodhound, from which it inherits its unusual head, long ears and low musical voice. Most probably, this dog gets its name from the French word *bas*, meaning low. Its short stumpy legs and deliberate gait made it an ideal dog for men hunting on foot.

Maybe, though, it got its name from its low and clarion-sounding voice, for bass is a musical term. Shakespeare refers to the basset in his play *The Midsummer Night's Dream*, as this breed was well-known even in the sixteenth century. His description of bassets at the hunt was no poetic flight of fancy. Their tuneful bays were a great booster to the morale of huntsmen.

Another hare hunting hound which is popular as a pet in Britain and the United States, is the beagle. It is an older dog than the basset and much smaller. It has short legs like the foxhound, and is often less than sixteen inches in height. Beagles have very sensitive noses and great stamina. When the other hounds are exhausted after a gruelling chase, the beagles are still fresh and ready to go on.

The foxhound, bred purely for hunting the fox, is not often kept as a pet today. They are kennelled in packs and a meeting of foxhounds and hunters is one of the few remaining examples of old time pageantry. The baying of the hounds, and the blasts of the horn are sounds which have stirred the pulse of the huntsman for hundreds of years.

Two lively Beagle puppies.

Photo: *Sally Anne Thompson*

A pack of Beagles setting out for the day's hunt.

Photo: *Wrexham Leader*

There are a number of different kinds of foxhounds. But they all have a tremendous capacity for sustained work. The foxhound has to keep up with his pack for many hours at a stretch in many kinds of weather, hot and tiring, wet and cold, and over many different kinds of terrain. Most schoolboys and athletes on a crosscountry run would find it impossible to put up such a long and difficult effort. But foxhounds are perfectly built for their job. They are intelligent dogs and become very attached to their masters.

There are many stories illustrating the devotion of foxhounds to their jobs and masters. One American bitch, called Bargain, always liked to be at the head of her pack. But one day her master noticed that she was missing.

When he searched for her back along the route, he found her entangled in a poacher's rabbit net, unable to get free. By the time he had freed her, he saw that the pack was so far ahead that they could not hope to catch it up.

But Bargain thought different. Nose to ground, she shot off in eager pursuit. Her master followed at a gallop, barely able to keep up with her. It was not long before the amazed huntsman saw Bargain overhaul the pack and take her rightful place at its head.

Few older types of hounds could have attained Bargain's speed. The fashion of chasing foxes on horseback was the main reason for breeding a faster hound. The fleet and cunning fox can cover great distances at a higher speed than the hare.

The foxhound in the United States has a shorter back and a racier appearance than the English types. The Southern

32

states, and especially Virginia, have close links with the development of the famous American foxhound. The English type foxhounds of the colonial era in the United States were crossed with fresh arrivals from Ireland and Europe. Some French hounds were sent to George Washington, who was an enthusiastic early breeder of dogs. The modern American foxhound is probably even faster over ground than the English colonial hounds, and just as intelligent.

At a demonstration during a summer outdoor show, one member of a pack, called Trotter, stopped and sniffed in the direction of a group of onlookers. A girl employed to look after the dogs, watching the show with her friends, was dismayed to see her favourite dog spoiling the display. The kennelmaid dared not shout at him and was relieved when he bounded back to rejoin his comrades.

Later, while enjoying a cooling soda with her friends, she was annoyed to feel a nudge at the back of her legs. When she turned round she was astonished to see an inquisitive hound standing by her side. The keen nose of the foxhound had recognized her smell—probably because there was no other competition on that particular day. The kennelmaid quickly returned him to the rest of the pack in case they all decided to join him.

There are many amusing stories told about the tricks played on the pursuing foxhounds by the wily fox. On one occasion, when a fox was being chased by a famous American pack it found a long roomy length of piping left behind in a field by some drainage engineers.

The fox stopped, and ran round the piping twice. Then it ran up and down inside it, before making off. When the hounds arrived at the piping, the fox's strong scent made them set up a terrific baying. Some of them ran around it in opposite directions. Others went in at both ends. As you can imagine, there was great confusion when the dogs met inside, all barking excitedly. Then, suddenly, to everyone's surprise, the piping began to move and rolled gently away down the field. When the huntsmen drew up in the field they found pandemonium let loose. No doubt that wily fox was secretly watching and enjoying the chaotic scene.

The low, short-legged dachshunds are popular in many parts of the world, although strictly speaking they are not really hounds. In Germany, they were used not only for going down badger holes, but also many wild boar expeditions included a small pack of dachshunds.

Queen Victoria of England received some dachshunds as a gift from a German prince. Her husband, Prince Albert, used them as retrievers when he went pheasant shooting in Windsor Forest. The Queen was very fond of her dogs, and there is no doubt that her affection for the dachshunds helped to make them popular in Britain and in many parts of the world.

They are certainly attractive as pets. Independent and brave, they have a cocky strut all their own. They are obstinate, self-important and know how to look after themselves. These proud little dogs are ideally suited to children, with whom they will romp for hours, provided that they are not roughly treated or made fun of.

34

There are many amusing stories about them. One dachshund, in a large kennel of dogs, was so sensitive to reprimands that if any dog were scolded, she took it to be a personal insult. As soon as she heard anyone speaking reproachfully, she would indignantly strut away to her own kennel, flop down in a corner in disgust, and would not come out unless she were wheedled.

Another dachshund was so hurt and upset by being dragged through a puddle of water, that he would never go out again in the rain, unless his owner carried him. But then many dachshunds view water with suspicion and distaste. If left to themselves, they will strut dignifiedly around it. If you try to force one of these independent little aristocrats to do something against its will, it will display a stubbornness that only great patience and understanding can overcome.

The dachshunds of the smooth-haired variety tend to be more cumbersome than the wire-haired and longhaired ones. The latter, probably because they are better protected by their coats, do not mind water and sometimes even like it. Toy or miniature dachshunds have recently become very popular in England and the United States. They often show an alertness and agility that one would not suspect these tiny, short-legged creatures were capable of.

Otterhounds have never had quite the same appeal as dachshunds. The true otterhound is about four times taller, and has a shaggy coat and furry face. They were first used in England during the reign of Henry IV. Later kings became so enthusiastic on hunting otters, which had originated in

France, that they imported otterhounds from the Continent. A special official to look after them was known as "Keeper of the King's Otter Hounds." These dogs had such a sensitive nose for otters that it was said that they could follow even a day-old track. But because this sport became less popular than other types of hunting, people have lost interest in this breed.

Salukis are much better known, though their size makes them too big to be popular pets today. They belong to the Borzoi group of dogs of which the Afghan hound is a famous member. Salukis were kept by the Arabs of Egypt and the Sudan, and were used as fast-running hunters. The Arabs did not hunt for sport, but for food. Until they began to use guns they were very dependent on these swift dogs to catch hares and tasty gazelles.

Because of this, Salukis were kept in very good condition. They were never overfed or allowed to put on weight. Some Arabs had their dogs strapped under the loins and stomachs so that they would feel uncomfortable if they ate too much.

The Arabs were nomads and so their dogs had to be hardy enough to endure a tough desert life. But they were loyal to their masters, and the Arabs have told many tales of dogs that have found their way back to their homes after being given away as gifts.

Salukis, like many lithe, fast running dogs, are "gaze" hounds, and hunt chiefly by sight. Although they can pick up a scent, they rarely put their noses to the ground like scenting dogs do. They stand and sniff delicately, almost invisibly,

A group of Salukis on the sea shore. These tall graceful dogs hunt chiefly by sight and can run at a very high speed.

Photo: *Sally Anne Thompson*

through their nostrils and then speed off in the direction of the scent until they glimpse their prey. A good Saluki, trained by Arabs, can overtake the swiftest of its victims after about three miles.

These tall graceful dogs are popular with Europeans living in the Middle East, who often take them on hunting and shooting trips. They describe the dogs as gentle and affectionate, docile and clean, and devoted to a family and home.

Like Salukis, deerhounds and other large hounds are not as popular today as smaller dogs. This is a pity as the Scottish deerhound is one of the most courteous of dogs. It is dignified and noble looking, while its loyalty would put many human beings to shame. It is a brave dog, a trusty dog. And, like so many of the best breeds, can only be coaxed, for it becomes unreliable and stubborn when handled by people who do not understand it. Although graceful, it cannot be described as handsome. Its temperament is its chief attraction.

Many people today object to deer hunting for sport, yet it requires great courage from the dogs. They need to be fit, quick and obedient if they are to be a match for fleet, agile, determined deer and hinds. The sport of hunting deer is far more organized now than it was a hundred years ago, especially in Scotland.

Lions and wolves were hunted by the Rhodesian Ridgebacks, borzois and, to a lesser extent, Afghan hounds, Rhodesian Ridgebacks, although little known in Britain, have a small but enthusiastic following in the United States. They are not an old breed, and did not become a special type until

38

early in the last century. They are called ridgeback because a ridge of hair on their backs grows in the opposite way to the normal growth of the coat. As a similar type of dog has been found on an island in the Gulf of Siam, it is likely that a seafaring expedition, including dogs, was once wrecked off its coast. A few of the dogs may have escaped drowning and swam to the coast.

Today's ridgeback is the result of crossing with hounds, mastiffs and terriers during the time when Europeans first settled in South Africa. The Dutch and English brought many dogs with them to use in hunting big game, either on foot or on horseback.

But what breed of dog, even when protected by guns, would face up to the fierce wild creatures of Africa? The merest "whiff" of a lion was enough to send most dogs speedily in the opposite direction.

The "king of the jungle" would never allow himself to be hunted like hares, foxes and deer. Hunting them, armed with either deadly spears or bullets, was a lengthy and tiring process.

These marauders usually prowled by night, and to track them with terrified dogs was a difficult problem. It was the ridgeback who came to man's aid. These curiously coated dogs possessed tremendous courage. They had the strength of mastiffs, could pick up a scent as well as any hound, and had the vitality and single-mindedness of terriers.

A Canadian sailor, called John Cameron, who spent some months training in South Africa early in the century, gives a first-hand account of their courage.

A large and wealthy party of overseas visitors had hired native bearers and guides for a lion shoot in the interior. They chose an area which could be reached by river so that they would not have to trek very far. One of Cameron's naval instructors owned a fast launch, which he offered to the safari, and he and Cameron were taken along as crew.

But they found their prey much sooner than they had expected. When two members of the shooting party started to carry some of their bedding off the boat into the jungle, they found their path barred by a lion. Cameron and his naval friend who owned a dog called Scout, were checking supplies below deck. Scout heard the lion's menacing growls and trotted up to the two terrified men. When he saw the lion the ridge of reverse-growing hair on his back stood up like bristles on a brush.

Then he barked. His rapid staccato brought the launch's crew bounding up on deck. There was something in its noise that was different from his usual cheerful excitement.

"Keep quiet. Keep still!" The naval officer had assessed the situation in a glance. "If the lion is parched with thirst it may attack. Then we'll dive for a rifle. But it might go away. Wait and see."

Then Scout's master spoke to the dog: "Good boy! Stay! Good boy. Speak—speak!"

On hearing his master's voice encouraging him to stay and bark, Scout moved in front of the two men and faced the majestic lion. The spectators thought they would be deafened by Scout's defiant barking and the lion's angry roars.

40

"Get as close to the launch as you can. If there's trouble, jump on board quickly."

The climax came a few seconds later, after the two men had backed up close to the launch. For, with a couple of gigantic bounds, the lion soared over the stationary dog toward them.

The plucky dog whipped around and leaped on the lion from behind.

"Quick! On to the boat!" Scout's master and some other men quickly pulled the two aboard. As soon as they were safe, Cameron rushed below for his rifle. His hands were trembling as he rammed in a clip of bullets.

"Don't fire until I can get Scout away from the lion. Get ready to cast off and move away."

And as the launch's engine started, it seemed to Cameron that they were abandoning the dog to its fate. He could hardly bear to watch.

"As soon as Scout gets free, shoot at the lion as fast as you can. I'll help you until the dog gets into the water. Then we'll switch off the engines and wait to pick him up."

Cameron's hands were sweating. Suddenly, the lion gave a terrific roar and a shriek. Scout had bitten either his tail or paw.

"Well done Scout, come on!" shouted his master.

John then knew it was time for him to act. Taking aim with his rifle, he fired three or four shots in quick succession. By the time Scout reached the river, the lion was dead. Five minutes later, he was on board, shaking the water off his coat and wagging his tail. It was not long before he was back in his usual position, at the stern.

Shooting on foot, as opposed to hunting on horseback, has produced another kind of dog, the gun dog. For many centuries, dogs were used to retrieve game for their masters. Guns first appeared in the fourteenth century, but it was some time before they were accurate enough to be used when shooting game.

The use of firearms affected the choice and breeding of dogs, as ones had to be found that would not be affected by sudden and disturbing noises. They had to be intelligent and patient enough to show where game was lying without scaring it off before the guns could be brought within range. They had to mark the game, by remaining still and pointing in the right direction. They had to be tall enough to be seen clearly through the grass and other vegetation. Setters and pointers were so named because of the nature of the duties for which they were trained.

However, because game very often lived in marshes, ponds, lakes, and streams, they usually dropped into the water when they were shot down. So special gun dogs were needed to retrieve their bodies. Spaniels, poodles and Portuguese water dogs were very good at this.

As time went by, rifles became more accurate and could be used efficiently at long ranges. Game was shot down so quickly and continuously, that fast-moving dogs were needed to pick it up. Cocker and springer spaniels were already known for their energy and enthusiasm in flushing out game.

The lively little cockers had been trained in wooded areas and were very skilful at bustling about in thick undergrowth, and even at penetrating under it. This made them especially useful at finding woodcock, which is how they got their name. The larger, springer spaniels were used on more open ground. They were powerful enough not to be put off by slopes and rocks, and earned their name because they could jump or spring from boulder to boulder.

There are so many different kinds of gun dogs, all renowned for their alertness and loyalty, that it is difficult to pick out the most popular one. In Britain and the United States, spaniels of all kinds, especially cocker spaniels, rate high in popularity, as do retrievers and setters.

One particularly famous dog in the United States is the American water spaniel, which is similar in appearance to a mixture of the curly coated retriever and the Irish water spaniel. As the Irish water spaniel was an offshoot of the Portuguese water dog—one of the oldest types of water dogs—there are many stories which link it with the voyage of Christopher Columbus. It is very likely that the Portuguese sailors had some type of water dogs with them.

The American water spaniel is not a big dog—spaniels are never very big—and it is an attractive chocolate brown. Its curly wiry coat is typical of water dogs. Like all spaniels, it is a good flusher of game and is patient and obedient. It is a good swimmer and will lie a long time in water, watching and waiting. Also these dogs are not put off or worried by the noise of shooting and can retrieve with uncanny speed.

Many dogs enjoy working in a stream or a pool but do not always like plunging into the sea. Newfoundland dogs are one of the few types that do. This noble and majestic dog is the true dog of sail. For they were the companions and helpers of the seafaring community after whom they were named.

In the olden days, steam sailing was often dangerous. Huge seas buffeted the slow-moving vessels, which pitched and tossed in the rolling waves. Then sailors discovered how useful big dogs could be. They often saved themselves from being swept overboard by holding on to their leads or collars.

Quite by chance a sailor, called Billy Robson, discovered another way in which Newfoundland dogs could be used.

He was mending some fishing nets on deck one day, when he was suddenly caught off balance as the ship listed to one side. Bill shot across the deck and dropped overboard into the sea. Fortunately, he was a good swimmer. But he had barely recovered from his surprise when something dropped into the sea not far away. To his amazement he recognized the large head of his pet Newfoundland, Roger. The dog was a wonderful swimmer, and soon he was splashing around him and licking his face. Bill had to grip his collar to control his excitement and stop his overwhelming affection.

Then Roger began to strike out toward the vessel whose crew were beginning to lower a boat. But it was hardly necessary for Roger was energetically pulling his laughing master back to the vessel.

As a result of this incident, the best of the Newfoundland dogs were trained to rescue seamen who had been swept over-

A Newfoundland dog. These plucky dogs enjoy plunging into the sea.
Photo: *Sally Anne Thompson*

board. They became world-famous for their exploits, and featured in a number of stories and paintings. It became quite common for ships to have a trained Newfoundland on board. The size and strength of the waves did not deter them. Men were saved from drowning, who although strong swimmers, had been knocked unconscious by the force of the mountainous waves. When a ship was in trouble, near the coast, a Newfoundland dog would swim for the shore, carrying a line to the rescuers.

Early in the nineteenth century an English brig, which had a Newfoundland and some puppies on board, foundered off the coast of Maryland. The English crew and their canine pets were rescued by an American vessel, the *Canton*. These rescued sailors had taken a terrible beating and were so grateful for being picked up that they gave two puppies, a dog and a bitch, as a present to the captain of the *Canton*. They were called Sailor and Canton.

The dogs settled in a home in Chesapeake Bay, and eventually bred with many of the local mongrels, which were used as duck retrievers. From this ancestry a remarkable retriever was bred, which is now a well-known dog in the United States. These retrievers have tremendous stamina and are such strong swimmers that a single dog is believed to have retrieved over 22 ducks in one day. The Newfoundland dogs' usefulness faded when sailing vessels were replaced by steam ones. Fishermen still find them valuable, but as they are too large to be kept as pets, the breed has waned.

The training and matching of animals against each other is

a hobby with the same appeal as racing motor cars, yachts and speed boats. Dogs are used for two types of racing—coursing, which takes place in the open and live hares are used, and greyhound racing, which takes place inside an enclosed terraced arena, and the hare is a mechanically-driven model.

Coursing, an ancient pastime, started in Britain in the eighteenth century, when it attracted many spectators, anxious for a flutter. It is less popular today, but one major event, the Waterloo Cup, for which the best dogs compete, draws many spectators to Liverpool.

After the end of the First World War, Mr. O. P. Smith, a farmer in Oklahoma, was fined for coursing a hare in his paddock. But he was determined to keep his dogs in training, and opened a circular track in Oklahoma City. It was an immediate success. Within a few years similar greyhound tracks were opened in other American cities.

In England, the first greyhound racing was held on a straight course near Hendon. The hare was a model worked by a hand-operated windlass. But the absence of bends made it almost certain that the fastest dogs would always win the race. Bends would have given a slower but clever dog the chance of passing them on the inside. Whippet racing, in which fast dogs were handicapped by starting at different points along the course, became more popular. Their track was about 200 metres long. A good dog could finish it in twelve seconds.

An American business man introduced the circular greyhound racing track into Britain, at Belle Vue, Manchester. It was very successful, although coursing enthusiasts did every-thing they could to discourage racing greyhound breeders from supporting it. They claimed that curves and the artific-ial hare would have a bad effect on the speed and interest of the dogs. But as these factors often resulted in a clever dog winning against a faster one, an element of uncertainty was added to the interest of the race.

Good greyhounds are very expensive, but it is possible to buy one cheaply and train it. Although a dog needs to be in peak condition and to have an expert training in order to reach high standards, this has been occasionally done by people who are far from wealthy.

One famous greyhound, called Mick the Miller, was bought from a Roman Catholic priest for £2,000, which was not considered a high price in the 1920's. He was bred in Ireland and had already won a number of races. Mick looked very ordinary, and would not have attracted much attention at a dog show. But he had a deep and thoughtful intelligence and was shrewd enough to watch other dogs, and adapt himself to the situation on the track. He could sense when the dogs would crowd at a corner and avoided them. He would look out for a space on the track and make toward it. He sometimes ran on the inside, but avoided it if the edges were slippery. Mick the Miller won 36 out of 40 races, and won the Greyhound Derby twice. At the age of five, when dogs retire, he beat all the popular young hopefuls in the 1930 St. Leger. These two races are the final ones of a series to find the fastest dogs in a particular year.

A greyhound being weighed in.

Photo: *Bolton Evening News*

There are many famous racing dogs in the U.S.A. Red Huntsman won the American Derby of 1950 and 1951, and is reported to have won over 60,000 dollars. Lucky Pilot, the record-breaker, was first 61 times out of 83 races. Indy Ann, a bitch, did even better than this, as she came first 137 times in her racing career. She was the outstanding American greyhound in 1955, 1956 and 1957.

All these dogs made their reputation because man trained them for his sport. Only the Newfoundland is an exception, and by the time of its rescues the nineteenth century had dawned. In the previous century—the eighteenth—harsh attitudes of men towards their dogs had reached its height. It is time to have a closer look at the dogs of this age and then find out what happened to change the relationship between dogs and people.

3: How Dogs Developed into Some Famous Breeds

Two centuries ago, animals were used mainly for carrying people, pulling vehicles, and providing entertainment. Those which were unable to do any of these things were regarded as being useless. They were probably the lucky ones. The demands on dogs were particularly harsh. They were given poor food and were usually expected to work until they dropped. Those that became sick were usually abandoned. They received no medical treatment, nor was it considered necessary that they should.

Some dogs were forced to do work which was quite alien to their natural instincts and temperaments. The revolving spit, a mechanical device for roasting meat, was often worked by dog power. Cooks disliked the intense heat of open fires and found it very tedious to continually turn a large roast so that it was browned all over. "Done to a turn" is an expression which goes back to the age of spits.

So small, long-bodied and crooked-legged dogs of non-descript appearance were imprisoned in a cage set into the wall near the fire. Inside the cage was a wheel, which when revolved, worked a rope which ran along pulleys to the spit. The dogs were trained to rotate the wheel at word of command, or when prodded. These little dogs were called turnspits.

Very large dogs, such as mastiffs, were used for haulage. Dog carts were used to carry one or two passengers from place to place at speed. These journeys often covered substantial distances and the dogs had to run for three or four hours without rest.

Dogs were used as entertainers by baiting other animals. They would tease monkeys, baboons, lions and bears to mention a few. These animals soon lost their tempers, thus adding to the fun. Audiences were deeply involved in this form of entertainment, and would cheer a brave attack or hiss at a dog which turned and ran away. Some spectators would become quite violent if they thought that the dogs weren't giving them good value for their money.

You would have seen an odd assortment of dogs at these entertainments. They were large and small, fast and slow, brave, cowardly or cunning. But this added spice and variety to the show. The dogs had to be chosen carefully if they were to stand up and fight a particularly fierce bull or bear. For a time, mastiffs or crossbreeds of large dogs were used against them. But it became increasingly necessary to use heavy, powerfully muscled dogs, with flat faces and strong jaws, which refused to give in.

Strong dogs were used for pulling people in small carts.
Photo: *Radio Times Hulton Picture Library*

Hence "bull dogs" were bred, to the delight of the spectators, who applauded their prowess in the ring. Their powerful haunches enabled them to launch a spring, and their fierce jaws could pin a bull by the nose. Bulldogs and terriers often attacked the bull in pairs. Sometimes teams of dogs would attack. Six or eight was the most common number in these teams. There was, of course, only one bull or bear!

The mastiffs, dogs and terriers matched against bulls became known as bull mastiffs, bulldogs and bull terriers. Over the years, their types became fixed and are now world-famous.

These breeds, and others, were also trained to entertain the public by competing with each other in rat pits or by direct combat against each other in dog fights. Rat pits attracted a very wide variety of people, for betting on a dog likely to win was a temptation few could resist.

The dog who could kill the most rats in a given time was the champion. Or the winner was the first dog to kill a rat. Highly-intelligent, quick-witted, clear-sighted, agile dogs were needed. Those chosen were usually the small and compact terriers, especially the fox and bull variety. Smaller dogs, such as cairns, Yorkshires and borders were also used.

Bull terriers were the best fighting dogs. In the Midlands of England, the white Staffordshires were bred only for their fighting qualities. These dogs were ruthless killers. They were ready to fight before they were even six weeks old. In other parts of the country, bull mastiffs and bulldogs also did well in the dog pits. Dog fights, which were as popular in the

54

Dogs being tossed while bull baiting.
Photo: *The London Museum*

United States especially in cities like New York and New Orleans, as in Great Britain, rarely finished with both dogs on their feet. In fact, an owner would not accept defeat until his dog lay motionless.

Farmers and farm workers liked good ratting terriers, bred from pit dogs. Then they would combine vermin control with sport. It was not an unusual sight to see men standing around a hayrick, holding terriers on leashes. A ferret would be released into the top of the rick and soon rats would be flying for the nearest ditch or hedge. The terriers were then released, to catch and kill them.

Terriers were used as sporting dogs, guards, and vermin killers for centuries, and automatically became pit fighters and ratters. They were known as fox terriers because of their skill in flushing out foxes and other small animals from rocks and crevices, where larger hounds were at a disadvantage.

The little steel-grey cairns, one of the oldest type of terriers, acquired their name because of their ability to nose their quarry out of caverns and cairns formed by fallen stones and boulders. Their owners would not allow them to be petted or fondled in case their ferocity and gameness was affected. These hard-working, perky, tough little dogs have a fantastic instinct, and can find their way home even when lost in the densest of fogs.

Another type of terrier was much sought after by wandering gypsies, tinkers and tramps. These rough-looking, long-bodied little dogs, with mustard or peppery hides were good at catching vermin, foxes and polecats, and were often sold as

The ratcatcher and his dogs.
Photo: *The London Museum*

puppies to farmers, One farmer, named Dandie Dimont, was a character in a story by Sir Walter Scott. He owned several of these little terriers. They so captured the readers' interest that they became known as Dandie Dimonts, a name which they have had ever since.

One terrier was given its name by a village in northern England, called Bedlington. The villagers used these terriers for tasks as varied as poaching, otter and badger hunting and dog fighting. This quick dog, a real jack-of-all-trades, also had to compete in racing and coursing. In order to breed a dog which could outspeed those who did nothing else but racing, they bred their terriers with whippets. Thus, we now have the Bedlington terrier, a graceful dog with something of the gazehound's appearance.

Another terrier is named after a city in the United States. A group in Boston decided to breed a dog which would combine the qualities of the bulldog and the terrier. A special dog, called Judge, which was a bulldog and a terrier cross, was imported from England and mated with other dogs. A French bulldog, especially, had a tremendous influence on establishing the new type. Forty local breeders decided to give the breed the name Boston terrier. At first, they were of many different sizes, but eventually, as small dogs were preferred, breeders concentrated on this point. The smart, well-built black and white Bostons are now one of the most handsome of the terrier breeds.

Sealyham terriers come from the same area of Pembrokeshire as Corgis, where a Captain John Edwards lived.

Captain Edwards had a burning ambition—to breed a really game and hard-working terrier. He did not care what it would look like. He only cared about what it would be able to do. It was not enough that it should be able and willing to work underground. Many dogs could do this. His terriers had to prove they were courageous as well. It was said that he never kept a dog for breeding unless it had tracked and killed a polecat. His dogs were all bred differently, too. He chose his blood lines from individual dogs. The only thing they all had in common was ruthlessness.

But today's Sealyhams only appeared after he had finished what he had set out to do. He merely laid the basis for this type by his experiments. He most probably would not have approved of the uniformity that the establishment of a breed is bound to acquire eventually. He liked to breed his Sealyham terriers from individual dogs.

Sportsmen of Norwich wanted to breed a terrier which could live indoors. A small sandy-haired dog, called Rags, was an important ancestor in the breed which later became known as the Norwich terrier. The Master and Whipper-In of the Norwich hounds kept and bred a number of perky looking terriers, which were very useful to the larger hounds when a fox had gone to ground. The Whipper-In, whose name was Frank Jones, bred and exported these attractive "Jones" terriers to many parts of the world.

Yorkshiremen living in the valley of the River Aire, liked to hunt the otter, and needed terriers that could also hunt the hares and rabbits that were so plentiful there. So they crossed their small black-and-tan local dogs with otter hounds. The dog they bred combines the qualities of hound and terrier, and is known as the Airedale terrier.

This black-and-tan dog is solid-looking, dignified and tall. Its high quality and reliability has made it invaluable as a police dog and protector of property.

Another famous terrier bred from the small black-and tan workers of Yorkshire is the renowned Yorkshire terrier. It is smaller than the Airedale and was bred as a result of crossing the black-and-tans with the silky coated Skye terrier.

A Boston terrier puppy.
Photo: *Purina Pet Foods*

4 : The Beginnings of Dog Welfare

It was not until the nineteenth century that the plight of dogs and other animals became the concern of the public. A clergyman, a hearty Irish politician, and a wealthy American were the three chief people who played an important part in the battle on behalf of the animals, in the cities of Liverpool, London and New York.

It was in Liverpool that announcements first appeared in the press asking people who were disturbed by the lack of concern for animals' welfare to attend a public meeting. As a result of the decisions made at this meeting, the first animal protection group was formed.

This group's success encouraged a young clergyman to try and form a similar group in London. London was then notorious for its animal entertainments and especially for the dog pit at Westminster.

The clergyman, the Reverend Arthur Broome, was modest

and patient. He had a powerful ally in Dick Martin, an Irish landowner and Member of Parliament, who was a clever orator. This hearty man, who was known as "Humanity Dick", loathed cruelty to cattle and other animals. Workers on his estate were forbidden to beat his herds. Broome enlisted his sympathy and interest and provided him with facts. He became Broome's mouthpiece and made many speeches exposing incidents of animal cruelty and exploitation. After one meeting, held in a coffee house in Old Slaughter Lane, in 1832, an organization was formed, which called itself the Society for the Prevention of Cruelty to Animals.

This victory was really due to the patience and planning of Arthur Broome. But the Society still needed help from the public and support from the government. A piece of good luck, or perhaps bold strategy, helped to win one, while Dick Martin's charm and persuasion in Parliament gained the other.

The Society wrote to Queen Victoria, who was known to be particularly fond of her collies, dachshunds and Skye terriers. They asked her if she would become a patron of the society. She agreed and, in 1840, the prefix Royal became part of its title. The S.P.C.A. was now the R.S.P.C.A.

Many Londoners decided to follow her example. People who had never considered dogs before were now anxious to follow the fashion. One London shopkeeper entered into the spirit by placing a bowl of water on the pavement outside his shop. It was marked "For dogs." His customers were greatly amused by his sense of humour. Nobody had ever before

A portrait of Dick Martin, the Irish politician, who fought
against cruelty to animals.

Photo: *The R.S.P.C.A.*

thought of putting down water for an animal. The bowl outside the shop drew a lot of attention and roars of laughter. The R.S.P.C.A., however, needed more than publicity. Cruelty to animals could only be wiped out when it was against the law and people could be punished for it.

After many attempts and much bitter opposition, Martin had some success, when a Bill was passed protecting cattle in 1822. In 1837 this was extended to all domestic animals. Even so, nobody really expected constables and magistrates to arrest and punish people for offences against animals. A man's property was his own affair and he could do what he liked with it.

However, eventually, the R.S.P.C.A. decided to employ men in plain clothes as inspectors. Wisely, they attacked dog baiting, dog fighting and dog carts first. Queen Victoria showed much interest in the R.S.P.C.A.'s work and gave her support to the inspectors. They had many difficulties to overcome. They often encountered fierce opposition, especially when a large crowd was watching a particularly exciting dog fight. After one brawl at a cock fight, in which an inspector was killed, badges of authority and truncheons were issued to them.

Then, some years later, a wealthy New Yorker, called Henry Bergh, who spent much of his time on sight-seeing tours paid a visit to London, and learned about the work of the R.S.P.C.A. He was a cultured man, who liked to write poetry and plays.

Bergh, then about fifty, realized that New York, although

Top: An early R.S.P.C.A. animal ambulance used between 1925 to 1931.
Below: Inside and outside views of the new R.S.P.C.A. mobile first aid unit.

Photo: *The Ford Motor Company*

so advanced in many ways, was very backward in the way it allowed animals to be treated. Stray dogs roamed the streets. Baiting and dog fights were common. Many store owners attracted shoppers to their windows by having dogs running on inclined treadmills, which worked animated advertisements. The dogs had to use their feet or become piled up in a heap at the bottom.

At first, Henry Bergh was alone and unaided in his work for animal welfare. But eventually his enthusiasm and determination gained support from many influential New Yorkers. As with the British pioneers, he was first concerned with the treatment of cattle and horses. But many of his efforts on their behalf were treated with derision. He was particularly worried by the dirty overcrowded conditions of the milking herds used by the New York dairies. One day, a reporter looking for a good story, asked him for an interview. The resulting article alarmed the women who feared these unhealthy animals might give infected milk to their children. Bergh was encouraged to bring cases to court. His evidence shocked New York. From that time, his views against animal cruelty were taken more seriously.

By 1866, the American Society for the Prevention of Cruelty to Animals had been founded. Seven years later, the American Humane Association was formed.

So, at last, a change took place in Britain and the United States in the relationship between dogs and people. Both animals and their owners have gained from this. Great strides have been made since the days of Broome, Martin and Bergh.

R.S.P.C.A. Inspector Bicknell with a terrier dog, which he rescued from the River Tame, Warwickshire. For this rescue, Inspector Bicknell received the R.S.P.C.A. Certificate of Merit.

Photo: *Birmingham Post and Mail*

Perhaps this new relationship is expressed best in a speech made by a former Senator from Missouri to a jury during a case in which a man had killed his friend's dog.

"When all other friends desert, he remains. When riches take wings and reputation falls to pieces, he is as constant in his love as the sun in its journey through the heavens. If fortune drives the master forth an outcast into the world, friendless and homeless, the faithful dog asks no higher privilege than that of accompanying him, to guard against danger, to fight against his enemies. When the last scene of all comes—there by his graveside will the noble dog be found, his head between his paws and his eyes sad, but open in alert watchfulness, faithful and true even unto death."

5: A Home for Lost Dogs and Medals for Brave Ones

Once again, events which were to have an important effect on dogs' welfare took place in London and New York. It was summer, and the year 1860, when a woman called Mrs. Major found a mongrel dog wandering through the streets of Islington, London. She could see that something was wrong with it. When she looked at it closely, she realized that the wretched animal was very hungry.

Mrs. Major, an animal lover, had a way with dogs. It wasn't long before the dog responded to her friendliness and began to wag its tail. She picked it up.

People stared in surprise at this well-dressed woman walking along the street, holding the dirty bedraggled creature in her arms. She didn't care. The mongrel nestled up close, looked up at her and occasionally licked her face.

When she reached home, she at once bustled into action. In no time at all, the mongrel was in her warm kitchen, eating a simple meal. While he was greedily lapping up the food, she found a big box which she made into a bed. By the time it was ready, the mongrel had licked its plate quite clean.

News of Mrs. Major's unconventional treatment of a mere dog travelled around. One of her friends, Mary Tealby, was most interested. She even called at the house to look at the mongrel while it slept. They were both delighted to see how peaceful and contented it looked.

Other women friends also came in to have a look at the stray dog. The idea of dogs being homeless worried them all. Some of these women were already helping the new R.S.P.C.A. in their spare time. Mary Tealby was anxious to do something really practical. Talking about helping animals was not enough.

"But what can just a few of us do in a large city like London?" one of the women asked.

"We can do what Mrs. Major has done. We can give a home to unwanted dogs," Mary Tealby replied enthusiastically. She was already becoming the leader of the group of friends. After a brief discussion, they decided they would write to the newspapers and try to get more people interested in the work of the R.S.P.C.A.

Mr. Tealby, her husband, took charge of the money raising side of the campaign. First he persuaded the women to write to relatives and as many friends as possible for donations. Money soon began to pour in, and they decided for the time being to postpone writing to the newspapers.

When they had enough money, the women opened a Home

for Lost and Starving Dogs in Holloway, London. To begin with, everthing went well. But it was a very costly venture. They soon became short of money and were obliged to write to the newspapers.

So an appeal to "the humanity of the ladies of London and its environs on behalf of the number of lost and starving dogs that are seen in the streets of the Metropolis" appeared in *The Times.*

People's reaction to their letter was swift and sympathetic. The editor of *The Times* confessed he could hardly believe his eyes. He felt that anybody who ran a Home for Lost Dogs must be mad. One reader, who lived just outside the city, poked fun at the writers. "If a Home had been formed for lost and starving dogs, why not a home of refuge for all the starving butterflies and caterpillars of the gardens of London?"

But the women of London were very sympathetic toward the idea. Money was sent in to help the crusade. Dogs were also taken to the Home. In fact, in the end, any dog seen wandering without a collar was carried enthusiastically to the Dogs' Home. As some of them had only wandered a few streets away from their home, many owners were surprised to find their pets there at all! Still, Londoners now knew where lost dogs would be given shelter, and many of them were glad to know where they could go if they did lose their pets.

The aim of this Home was to give shelter to dogs which where genuinely lost, or which had no homes. Policemen on their lonely patrols at night often picked up strays. Now they knew they could take them to the strays' Home at Holloway.

This was a great relief as before that the policemen had not known what to do with some of the dogs they picked up.

By 1870, the Dogs' Home was a flourishing concern. Nearly 10,000 dogs a month were taken in, and there were usually about two hundred dogs living there at a time. But this busy dog shelter was not too popular with local residents, who were often annoyed by the noisy barking. It was not long before the Dogs' Home began to receive complaints about the noise.

So the following year, the Home moved to a new building in Battersea. But as soon as the dogs were settled there new troubles arose—rabies! This horrible disease, to which dogs are so susceptible, swept like wildfire through the country's dog population. Its deadly infection, carried by germs in the dog's saliva, can be passed on to human beings if they are bitten by an infected dog. Because of this, the police were worried that children might be bitten. They took all stray dogs they found to the Dog's Home. Regular searches for stray dogs were organized.

Within a few years of this outbreak, the Dogs' Home was struggling to look after thousands of dogs. In one year alone, 42,614 stray dogs were received. The few that had rabies were isolated from the others. But the great majority of the dogs were perfectly normal and healthy animals.

Some people thought that all the dogs had rabies and believed that the staff were very courageous to look after them. As all the dogs were very well cared for, Londoners came to respect the work of the Home.

A porter and inmate of the Battersea Dogs' Home.

Photo: *The R.S.P.C.A.*

Today, the Battersea Dogs' Home is a well-known British institution, which has cared for more than two million dogs. As a result, many dogs have been spared the unhappiness of being deserted and neglected. A few from the Home have even achieved fame. One fox terrier sold for a small price to a big game hunter and photographer, became the hero of a book called *My Dog Simba*. Another, a black retriever, was the pet of a Deputy Commissioner in Burma. He saved his master's life when he was attacked by a band of thieves and murderers.

We no longer regard this kind of devotion as unusual. Dogs have responded to human friendship and have shown that there is more in them than people had ever realized. Some of the stories of their loyalty and heroism are almost beyond belief.

During the First World War, a soldier stationed in England was allowed to have his pet dog Chips—a black and white terrier—with him in his quarters. But when he was posted overseas to France with his unit, he was not allowed to take Chips with him. His pet could not bear to be without his master and could not settle with any other owner.

Then, six months later, in the middle of a bitter, snowy winter, the soldier saw a half-starved, utterly exhausted dog dragging its way toward his trench. Under its filth he noticed it had a black-and-white coat.

The soldier stared closer, unable to believe his eyes. It couldn't be. . . it was! The dog bounded up to him, its wretchedness forgotten as he greeted him in a way that only

Many brave dogs' names are inscribed in this book; a few have won this silver medal.

Photo: *The P.D.S.A.*

Chips could. His dog had crossed the channel, and somehow found his way up to the front line. How he had done it was beyond explanation. Somehow his loyalty and devotion had triumphed over all obstacles.

But even more surprising than a dog's loyalty to his owners are the risks that some people will take to help a dog.

There is the case of the American, John Doerflinger, for instance, which took place before the beginning of the First World War. John Doerflinger heard a dog whimpering somewhere along the track of New York's overhead railway. Most men would have ignored it. But Doerflinger wanted to find out what was the matter. He knew that the whimper was a distress signal that could only come from a frightened or injured dog. He tried to rescue the dog and, in doing so, was himself injured. Doerflinger was taken to a hospital and the newspaper stories created a big sensation out of the story. For it then seemed incredible that a man should risk his death for the sake of a mere dog.

At that time members of the American Humane Association were holding a convention in New York. This Association was originally founded in Cleveland, Ohio, in 1877–78 to improve the conditions of animals in transit between east and west. They were very moved to hear of Doerflinger's courage and were also impressed by the wide publicity his act had received. They decided that in future such deeds of heroism would be rewarded by a medal. This was to be named the Stillman Award named after one of their most active Presidents. It could be earned by animals as well as human beings. There was Gretchen, a handsome Weimaraner dog, who received this award in California, in front of a very large audience. Many people were anxious to see the dog which had performed such an incredible feat of bravery.

In July, 1961, Gretchen was travelling in a car with her master, Ramon Miller, along a lonely road through the Mojave Desert, toward Death Valley, California. Miller had been involved in a motor accident some years earlier, and had lost a leg. This fact was very much in his mind when the car broke down. It was blazing hot and he knew he could not walk far with his artificial leg. Still, there was nothing wrong with his vehicle, it was just that it had run out of fuel.

Unfortunately, the road was completely deserted. This meant they would have to walk to get help. So for seven long hours, Ramon Miller and his dog trudged slowly back along the road. Completely exhausted and parched with thirst, it was not until the next day that they found water. By then, Miller could walk no further. His sound foot was blistered and raw from walking, and he needed hours of rest before he could continue. So, finding a cavern near to the water spring, Miller crept inside to shelter from the heat.

After the sun went down, the wild animals came to the spring to drink. Finding Miller and his dog, they attacked them. Miller could not stand up and defend himself; he was an easy prey.

However, Gretchen had no intention of allowing these creatures to harm her beloved master. Snarling and barking ferociously, she drove them away. By morning, both dog and

77

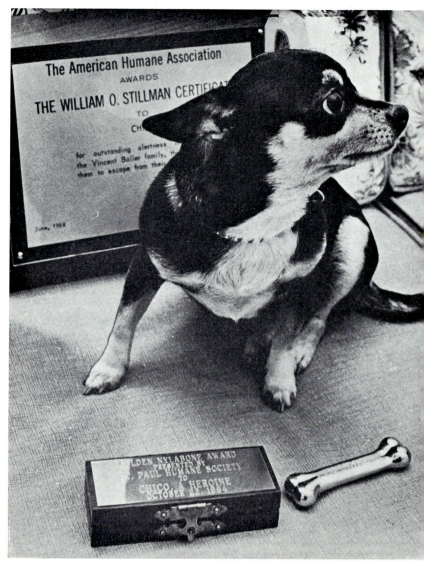

Chico, the alert chihuahua, and her award.

Photo: *Minneapolis Tribune*

man were in a state of collapse. Gretchen was exhausted by her exertions, and Miller through lack of sleep and anxiety. Every night for a week the courageous dog protected her crippled master and drove off the animals' attacks.

Then, on the seventh day, they were found by two men, who had come across the abandoned vehicle on the road! Miraculously, although injured and weakened through lack of food, both Gretchen and Miller recovered from their ordeal. The dog was badly bruised and torn by her fights with the wild animals. Even so, she has since had a litter of five sturdy puppies. Her master gave one to each of the two men who rescued them from the cavern.

Another and more recent Stillman Award winner was Chico, an attractive little chihuahua dog, through whose efforts four human beings were saved from being burned to death.

Vincent and Elizabeth Baller and their two daughters, Kathie and Cheryl, led a quiet life in East Avenue, St. Paul, Minnesota, a rather pleasant residential American city.

However, if you had been around early one June morning, you would gave seen the entire family, dressed in their night clothes, standing on the pavement in front of their blazing house. They were waiting for the fire engines to arrive.

They did not have to wait long. Soon, with sirens screaming, two fire engines roared down the quiet street to put out the fire.

The family was lucky to have escaped with their lives. And they owed their escape to Chico. The little dog, who slept in

F

the girls' room, had barked and barked so insistently and excitedly that the girls woke up, sat up and sniffed.

It was not long before they realized the house was on fire. By the time they had awakened their parents, they had to force their way through smoke and flames to reach the safety of the street. The fire had been building up for some time for, as soon as they were outside, one side of the house was gutted by the flames.

The firemen, who appeared very swiftly on the scene, estimated that within another five minutes, the family would have been suffocated by the smoke or burned to death. They had come out just in time.

Other dogs have received the Stillman Award for preventing their owners from being burned to death. Two of these were a couple of Pekingese, with the rather charming names of Sen Su and Penny Sing Lee. Sen Su and Penny Sing Lee were sleeping together in the kitchen when they smelled the fire. They, too, raised the alarm by their insistent barking. As it was something they rarely did, their mistress awakened to find that her bedroom was filled with smoke. Strangely enough, Sen Su's cousin, another dog, had also saved his mistress's life when her bedroom was gutted by fire. Unfortunately, he died later from his own severe burns.

Another Stillman Award, this time to a human, was for a rescue from water rather than from fire. It took place in Rome, Georgia, on a bitterly cold and icy January day. There was an eight-inch snowfall on the ground. Even so, things were comparatively quiet at the County Sheriff's

Office. Then the phone rang. The caller wanted to know how to rescue a dog from a deep well. Joe Adams, the Sheriff, decided that it was too risky a job for an inexperienced person to undertake. He decided to go himself. He stopped first at the Fire Department to pick up the Fire Chief and his assistant.

When they arrived on the scene, they were met by an almost hysterical crowd of people. Apparently, in an attempt to rescue her pet dog from the well its young and attractive owner had fallen in, too. The dog had walked over the wooden cover of the well, and fallen in when one rotten plank had given way. It had dropped down into 75 feet of water in a 100 foot deep well. Badly frightened, it had managed to keep its head above the water and made a tremendous amount of noise for its size.

Helped by her children, the dog's mistress lowered a wicker basket in the hope that the dog would crawl into it. But it did not seem able to do so. So, in her anxiety the young woman leaned too far over the edge and fell head first into the water, banging her legs and thigh against the side of the well.

She could not help the dog now, nor for that matter herself. Her legs were useless, and she was having great trouble to keep afloat. A ladder was lowered for her to cling to, but the woman refused to be rescued until her dog was safe.

"This is the first time I've ever rescued an animal before a human being," exclaimed the Fire Chief in amazement.

So a rope was lowered and the woman tied it around the

dog's body. When the dog was safely out of the well, the men turned their attention to its mistress. When she was, finally, pulled out she was in such pain that she could not walk, and had to spend nearly a week in hospital before she could get around again. Had not the Sheriff and his assistants arrived when they did, she would have died. So this woman and her three rescuers all received the Stillman Awards.

In Great Britain, other notable awards have been given by the People's Dispensary for Sick Animals. Rusty, a golden cocker spaniel, had his name on the Animals Roll of Honour. This affectionate and intelligent animal helped an invalid child to recover the use of her limbs and her power of speech.

The gentle and playful dog encouraged the small child to crawl. The game he played with her everyday eventually resulted in the child being able to stand upright and toddle across the room. She was also making efforts to try and speak when, alas, her faithful canine friend died of old age.

Another dog, a golden retriever called Jane, saved a child's life. Jane was standing with her owner, waiting to cross a busy road, when she heard a cry of alarm from a woman nearby, whose child had stepped into the highway in the path of a fast-moving car. The dog instantly sprang forward and seized and dragged the child back. There was barely a second to spare.

So dogs have shown themselves to be alert, intelligent and brave. They are also faithful. In September, 1967, after a ten hour search, in rain, sleet and gale force winds, a Welsh mountain rescue team found the body of a missing climber on

Tip, who guarded the body of her master through fifteen weeks of moorland winter.

Photo: *John Lawson Reay*

a high peak. Standing guard over its master was a brown-and-white spaniel. It refused to move from its position until the body was picked up. Only then did it allow itself to be led away on an improvised leash.

Tip, an eleven year old collie bitch, also guarded the body of her dead master, an eighty-six year old shepherd, through fifteen weeks of severe moorland winter, although she was weak from exposure and lack of food.

Trained dogs are required in certain types of rescues, such as searching for a lost child or missing person, or cases when avalanche dogs are needed to find a person buried under snow. In these cases, trained police dogs and handlers are rushed to the scene.

Pet dogs often perform brave deeds on their own, without any instruction. Not all dogs, of course, possess the courage, intelligence or physique of the award-winning dogs. The Weimaraner had both the courage and the strength to save her master, while the little chihuahua was able to use her intelligence in a situation which did not require any strength. Both these dogs possessed devotion, without which the outcome would have been very different.

The growing number of entries of such brave deeds would have surprised earlier generations. The presence of names of humans, who have saved dogs, would have probably suprised them, too. Even now, although the idea of humans loving dogs and dogs being devoted to their owners is accepted, people can still be amazed when they read about a dog's courage and loyalty.

6 : Care for Sick and Injured Dogs

Veterinary knowledge and skill were limited until the First World War. People did not know how to treat the sicknesses and injuries suffered by animals. During the War, however, dogs and horses, so useful in the front line, were often wounded and needed first aid. Also, the submarine blockade of Britain made it necessary to protect the cattle herds used for food. So veterinaries were recruited for service on the home and battle fronts.

Conditions on the battlefields were appalling. There was an acute shortage of equipment and essential supplies. But many of the veterinaries were so dedicated to the cause of animal welfare that they amazed and impressed the soldiers. Lieutenant Paul George, a French Canadian, was such a man.

It was a cold, wet night in France. Patrols from the German and Allied sides had been very active, and they were both accompanied by dogs. When dawn broke, the German soldiers were still out and had suffered a few casualties. Eventually, when they managed to return to their own lines, they discovered that the handler's German shepherd dog had been wounded and lost. The handler was very fond of his animal and his comrades had great difficulty in preventing him from going back to search for it.

Shortly after returning to their own lines, troops in the Allied New Zealand sector heard moans coming from No Man's Land. The officer in charge, realizing that they were being made by an animal, sent a message to the rear calling for a veterinary surgeon.

It was an hour before Paul George arrived. By then, all the men knew that the moans were coming from a dog, and that it could only be a German one, as none of theirs was missing. The New Zealand officer apologized to Paul George saying, "There's no need to rescue a German dog."

But he was due for a surprise. Lieutenant Paul George had been a veterinary surgeon in his civilian occupation. He was one of the few "horse doctors", as they were called, and was kept very busy visiting sectors held by soldiers from many parts of the world. He regarded all animals as his friends, and felt that it was his duty to help them, regardless of whether they belonged to German or Allied troops.

Paul did not listen to the New Zealand officer's remarks. It was enough that he had heard the cry of an animal in distress. He took off his heavy overcoat and helmet, which he knew would get in his way, rolled up his sleeves, and picked

Many dogs were used in the front line during the First World War.
Top: Laying wire.
Bottom: Carrying a message.

Photo: *Imperial War Museum*

up the canvas bag which held his medical supplies. Without a thought of danger, he climbed out of the trench and ran forward, keeping as low down as he could. He was used to finding animals, and soon he was moving in the direction of the dog's whimpers, ducking every now and then to avoid a stray shot.

The German officers were curious about the lone figure which they could see through their field glasses. What was the man holding in that bag? Was it grenades? Was he going to repair some wire on a trench? But why did he expose himself to such danger?

Just as they were about to open fire on him, the man disappeared down into a shell crater. They waited, ready for him to appear.

The delay puzzled them. Why was he taking so long, and what was he doing? Perhaps he was a man made crazy from shell shock!

Paul, of course, had found the dog. It tried to bark at him when he dropped into the crater, but the dog was too weak from a head wound. Fortunately, the bullet had only nicked open a large gash at the side of the head, and the dog was suffering mainly from loss of blood. Paul had somehow to clean the wound and then stitch the open skin together to reduce the bleeding. He would then try to stop the bleeding altogether by pressing on its neck.

The dog soon trusted him. Paul was a good doctor and was also strong. Even so, he was exhausted by the time he had finished his task, and had no sedative to give to the dog to calm

German dogs receiving treatment.

Photo: *Imperial War Museum*

Bandaging a despatch dog wounded in the head at a dogs' hospital behind
the line, March 1918.

Photo: *Imperial War Museum*

it. If he could find its master then the dog, feeling safe would fall asleep.

There was no point in carrying the dog back to the Allied lines. Somehow, Paul had to make the Germans understand that their help was needed and that the Allied troops would cease fire for a while. So he tied a white bandage around his arm and waved another bandage above the crater. Both the New Zealand officer and the German officer were watching through their field glasses. Everything was quiet when Paul rose slowly above the crater. He could see the soldiers on both sides gazing in his direction.

He decided to stand upright and shout out the only German word he knew: "*Kamerad!*" Then he strolled determinedly toward the enemy lines. He had made a mental note of the dog's name and number which were on its collar. When he arrived at the German position he pointed back to the crater and kept repeating, "1,826—Karl!"

At once understanding flashed across a corporal's face, and things began to move fast. The corporal called for the dog's handler. Then three men made their way toward the crater. As they drew near to Paul, the New Zealand officer and his orderly also climbed out of their trench. Soldiers from both sides were watching expectantly.

When finally Karl was lifted out, there was a storm or whistling, clapping and cheering from both sides. After many handshakes, Paul returned to the Allied lines. He now knew that the dog was in safe hands again.

There was a sequel to this strange incident. One week later, white flags of truce were waved by the Germans. After a minute or so, a soldier and a German shepherd dog scrambled out of their dugout and walked up and down the line in full view of everyone. The applause was spontaneous. All the soldiers were glad that Karl was fit and well again.

The dog was cured because his wound had not been exposed too long, and the bleeding was stopped. Fifty years earlier a neglected injury would probably have proved fatal. There was no electricity for warmth and light, and neither antibiotics nor drugs. An animal had little chance of surviving a serious injury. Nowadays, the most extraordinary recoveries are made and nobody thinks anything of it.

Brandy, a working collie in the north of England, had four spinal discs treated by a university department of a hospital. Before her operation she had lost the use of her back legs and was unable to walk. One disc was removed and the others moved and repositioned. She was then immobilized in a plaster cast. Her farmer owners were told to keep her that way as long as they could. Only time would repair the damage.

Brandy was a very active dog. It had been her job to move the cattle between the cattle sheds and fields every morning and night. She also kept a watch on the farmhouse and outbuildings and gave warning when strangers approached.

She loved her work and, although her owners took good care of her and had a bed for her in the farm kitchen, she wanted to be out with the cattle. She made such a fuss, whining and whimpering, that she had to be carried over to the cattle shed and placed in a window where she had a good view of the herd as it moved along the lanes. She watched the cows being milked and saw them being "strawed in" at night. As Brandy had to be carried back to the kitchen for her meals, her owners soon became exhausted at having to lump this hefty dog around. So they made a trolley on which they could wheel her. When Brandy guessed that she was going to be pushed around the farm just like an invalid, it was the last straw. She knew it was time for her to get better, and get better she did!

Another dog, an Irish setter and spaniel cross, called Prince, who lived in the Bronx, a borough of New York, had a similar trouble to Brandy. His back legs became paralysed and he was unable to walk. After treatment by a veterinary surgeon, Prince showed no improvement and had to submit to an operation. A spinal disc, which had been affected by a calcium deposit, was successfully removed. Then his back and loins were put in plaster. The dog would not be able to bear the weight of his large heavily-coated body until new tissues had formed.

Prince was luckier than Brandy as only one, not four, of his discs were in plaster. He was able to do without the cast in about a week but, as he still could not carry his weight, he had a two-wheeled cart fixed around his loins. He soon became so expert at moving about on his two front legs, dragging his lifeless back ones behind him, that his paws became sore. His owner was, eventually, obliged to put them into a pair of rubber boots.

Distemper was the great scourge of dogs until the middle

Care for Sick and Injured Dogs*

of the twentieth century. They suffered for many weeks before they reached the final convulsion stage, which was quickly followed by death. This disease, caused by an air borne virus, was highly contagious and could spread swiftly through a community, killing most of the dogs infected by it. A dog could catch it merely by visiting a spot where the virus had been.

It was in the 1950's that the first breakthrough against this disease came. A vaccine, made up of weakened live distemper was inoculated into dogs to give them immunity. Shortly after, dogs could be given protection against infectious hepatitis, a disease of the liver. Recently another vaccine against fatal jaundice (leptospirosis) has been added. Now a dog may be immunized against all these three diseases with only a single inoculation.

Many diseases which ten years ago would have destroyed millions of puppies, can now be cured. Miracles of surgery have been performed on dogs. Legs have been replanted, even after they have been severed for several hours. Glue is used in place of stitches in many canine operations. Few blood transfusions were made twenty years ago. Now many veterinarians maintain blood banks, and transfusions are frequently made.

At one time, dislocated knee joints could not be cured in tiny dogs. Now surgeons can, quite easily, cure this condition. Missy, a tiny four month old black toy poodle, underwent this operation at the University of Pennsylvania Veterinary School. Afterwards, she was fitted with splints to hold the repairs in place, and with model airplane wheels to enable her to move around. When the splints and the wheels were removed after four weeks, little Missy was able to use her rear legs.

Fractures in dogs can now be easily cured. Dogs are no longer immobilized for weeks, with plaster casts covering half their body. Surgeons have learned how to pin and brace the healing bones internally, so that casts no longer have to be used.

Many dogs suffer from heart complaints. When five thousand dog patients were examined at a university veterinary clinic, it was discovered that about a tenth of them had some sort of heart defect. As the disease becomes worse, with age, one third still showed a heart ailment when examined later. Heart failure was twice as high in male dogs as in female ones, and was also, strangely enough, very high among cocker spaniels.

Digitalis* was used for dogs with heart failure over a century ago, before, in fact, it was used for humans. Veterinarians now prescribe cage rest and salt free diets. This is because animals suffering from heart failure have to be forced to rest in cages, while lack of salt in their diet lowers their energy and reduces their blood pressure. But in many cases, only some sort of operation can cure the dog.

Melissa, a cocker spaniel, was handicapped from birth by a defective heart, and she underwent an operation to repair the blood spillover defects caused by leaking arteries that

* Medicine prepared from foxgloves

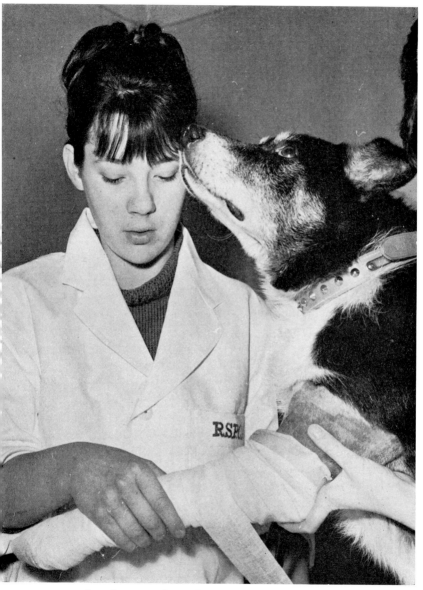

A patient at an R.S.P.C.A. clinic, Putney, London.

Photo: *Keystone Press Agency Ltd.*

were robbing her of her vitality. The most up-to-date equipment was used during the operation. There was an oscillascope to monitor her pulse and breathing, blood was carefully typed to match the patient's own, and a diagnostic radiograph, rather like a sort of instant X-ray was used to guide the surgeon in making the repair.

The surgeon had to work on a heart the size of a lemon, and on arteries whose diameter was no thicker than a cigarette. The operation was successful. Five years ago any exertion caused her to pant excessively. Today, Melissa is a healthy bouncing dog.

Veterinary surgeons have to reach a very high standard. Their training is as intensive as that of a physician.

Pets travelling in vehicles with their owners can often be victims in road accidents. Ambulances are swiftly summoned to the scene to the aid of the humans. But it is only in some of the larger cities of Great Britain and the United States that there are ambulance services for animals. Vehicles of the A.S.P.C.A. and the R.S.P.C.A. in London, Liverpool and New York, are equipped with two way radio sets. Sometimes some strange messages are transmitted between the wireless operators at headquarters and the drivers in the streets.

One morning, a driver of a New York A.S.P.C.A. vehicle received a message that a lost and frightened mongrel puppy had taken refuge under a large car. Nobody could manage to entice it out. The driver of the radio car raced to the place. Then, by lying flat on his stomach on the pavement, he managed to lasso the dog and drag it out.

An A.S.P.C.A. chauffeur reports the finding of a lost dog.
Photo: *The A.S.P.C.A.*

There have been many other rescues by the A.S.P.C.A. Once they had to rescue a litter of mongrel puppies which had been accidentally sealed up behind a freshly plastered wall. Another time, a large handsome dog had fallen into a partially dug hole on some wasteland in Harlem. It was rescued, given veterinary care, and quickly recovered. All this concern for the suffering of animals would have seemed incredible to the public of a hundred years ago. So the societies, which were founded to work for animal welfare, have much to their credit.

7 : Famous Dogs and Famous People

Because of the new humane approach to dogs, people began to notice the grace and beauty of certain breeds. This led to exhibitions of dogs at shows. The winning dogs, which had been tended with such care, made owners aware of how good grooming improved dogs, and made them pay attention to the condition of their coats, mouths, eyes and ears. Books on dogs—breeding, feeding and treatment for illness—became popular.

The founder of one of the world's greatest dog shows was Charles Cruft. He started his career in London, where he sold "dog cakes," which were really ship's biscuits. His employer, James Spratt, had just returned from the United States, where dog cakes had been invented after a supply of ship's biscuits had been eagerly bought by dog owners.

Cruft travelled around the large estates in England, where packs of hounds were kept for hunting. The business flourished and in 1878 he went to France to sell biscuits. There he was approached by French breeders who wanted him to organize a canine section for the famous Paris Exhibition.

Because of this tribute, British breeders asked Cruft to help organize their own dogs shows. This Cruft did, but he was not content to remain behind the scenes, and soon began to hold shows of his own. He called them Cruft's Shows. By the turn of the century, dog shows and the name Cruft were inseparable. After his death in 1938, the Cruft's Dog Show was such a big project that his widow did not think she could manage to hold any more on her own. So now Cruft's Shows are held under the auspices of the Kennel Club and are becoming more and more popular.

Many people criticize dog shows because they believe that beauty rather than intelligence is the main consideration. Although this is partly true, they do provide models for owners to copy.

Dog admirers enjoy watching the graceful dogs as they stand erect, or walk up and down the ring for the judges to appraise them. Dogs and people find pleasure in being together. The public wander from breed to breed, and compare them with their pets at home. The dogs don't mind. Perhaps some are bored, but most of them enjoy the fuss and attention they receive. All the dogs are at their best, alert and dignified, and proud to be there.

Many people, such as owners of canine winners of national and international dog shows and greyhound races, have achieved some sort of fame for themselves through their dogs.

Judging deerhounds and borzois at Cruft's Dog Show.
Photo: *Radio Times Hulton Picture Library*

A few owners have been brought into the news through some unexpected exploit of their dog.

There was the case of the British dog, Pickles, who found the famous World Cup, the Jules Rimet trophy for football, which had been stolen a few months before the nations were to compete for it. The dog's inquisitiveness on a walk with his master about an object wrapped up in paper on a garden verge, led to the cup being found. This brought publicity and a large reward to its owner.

Then there was Sandy. Sandy was a celebrity dog of Cooperstown, New York. He could solve fractions and various mathematical problems by giving the correct number of barks. One day Sandy had wandered away from his owner on to a railway track, where he had been caught on a spike by his lead chain. He could not move and stood right in the path of a heavy locomotive pulling a freight train. Fortunately, he was spotted by the young fireman. The driver blew a warning blast on the engine's whistle, but Sandy could not move. So, quick as lightning, the fireman jumped off the engine and raced to Sandy's side. He grabbed the dog off the spike and flung him back across the tracks just before the locomotive rumbled past. Because of Sandy's mathematical fame, the fireman found himself and the dog featured in many newspaper articles.

On the other hand, many dogs have become famous because they belonged to well-known people. The renowned novelist Sir Walter Scott, was a great dog lover. Camp, a bull terrier, was a most beloved pet. He was also very fond of his two

Pickles, the dog who found the World Football Cup, with his master.
Photo: *The Press Association Ltd.*

greyhounds, Douglas and Percy, who shared his fireside. Even in winter, he would leave his study window open, so that the dogs could run in and out as often as they liked. Camp, determined and courageous, yet gentle with children, was like a human friend to him. This great writer held conversations with him as if he were speaking to one who understood. Douglas and Percy were amusing creatures whose pranks he enjoyed, but Camp was an equal.

When the dog grew old, he was not always able to accompany his master on his long walks. Even so, he always tried to meet him as he returned to the house. Sir Walter Scott was stricken with grief when the faithful old dog died.

As well as the bull terrier and greyhounds, Scott was very attached to a setter, called Finette, and a staghound called Maida. Maida was a dignified and courtly dog, while Finette liked a game. She would often bound on to Maida hoping for a good chase. A growl and a bark were enough to scare her off.

Maida and Scott were completely devoted to each other. Scott had only to snap his fingers for the great dog to leave the hearthrug and lay his head across his master's knee, waiting to be fondled.

In a letter to a friend, Scott summed up his own feelings for dogs: "I have sometimes thought of the final cause of dogs having such short lives, and am quite satisfied it is in compassion to the human race: for if we suffer so much in losing a dog after an acquaintance of ten or twelve years, what would it be if they were to live double that time?"

A memorial to his beloved dog, Maida, in the grounds of Sir Walter Scott's home.

Photo: *Radio Times Hulton Picture Library*

The British royal families have always been very attached to their dogs and horses. This was especially true of the Stuarts. Charles II advertised for his lost dog, "A black dog, between a greyhound and a spaniel." He believed that it had been stolen. Charles, rather pro-French, stressed that the dog would never leave him of its own accord because it was too loyal and it was not English.

The King's fondness for "foreign" spaniels caused much talk in London. He used to take them for walks through St. James's Park every morning. Some Londoners thought that the King could have used the time better looking after the affairs of the country.

Prince Rupert, another Stuart, was very fond of dogs. When his dog, Boy, was killed at the battle of Marston Moor, he wrote, "I would rather have lost the best horse I own." This view was unusual for that period, for few men then would have compared the loss of a dog with that of a horse.

At her execution, Mary, Queen of Scots, wept when she saw her faithful little dog being dragged away from her. It returned later to keep vigil over her body.

Queen Victoria was, of course, the first British monarch to concern herself with the welfare of dogs. She kept about seventy dogs of different breeds in her kennels at Windsor Castle and they were all well looked after. The Queen liked to feed the dogs herself, and would never allow one to be destroyed just because it was ill. She insisted on it being nursed and cared for.

Queen Victoria with her dog, Sharp, at Balmoral, 1867.
Photo: *Radio Times Hulton Picture Library*

When it became fashionable to clip the dogs' tails the Queen had too much respect for their feelings to follow the current fashion. Tails were docked in many fighting breeds so that their opponents could not seize them and throw them off balance. This "masculine" fashion spread to other breeds. Many people were astonished at the way she reacted to her dogs' deaths. Each dog had its own grave, which was decorated with flowers. Deckel, a dachshund, even had a memorial headstone.

When the British and French forces entered Peking in 1860, a Pekingese dog was presented to Queen Victoria. This little creature, which was named Looty, must have seemed a strange and ugly animal to people then. But the small, frail queen especially loved little dogs and became even more attached to them as she got older. This queen, in whose reign so many great issues were determined, had a little Pomeranian beside her when she died.

Queen Elizabeth the Second grew up with Rex, an affectionate golden Labrador. She was always fond of corgis— Little Jane, Crackers, and Carol, were three belonging to her family. Crackers died in 1953. During his illness, he was taken outside in a miniature push chair so that he could have fresh air. Rikki, a tiny dachshund, also owned by the Queen Mother, once caused great excitement when she had to be rushed in a fast car well over a hundred miles for an X-ray at Inverness in Scotland.

Queen Elizabeth owns four corgis. Buzz and Heather, two of them, are the children of a corgi owned by the Queen

H.R.H. Prince Andrew with one of the royal corgis.

Photo: *Studio Lisa Ltd.*

The dachshund, Rikki, and the corgis, Bill and Bee, belonging to the British royal family.

Photo: *Studio Lisa Ltd.*

Mother, called Bee. Foxy and Tiny are Heather's children and were born in 1965. Prince Charles and Princess Anne also have two corgis, Whisky and Sherry, which they were given in 1955. The royal dogs and children have often caused amusing hold ups at railway stations during royal departures for the country. There is no doubt that the Pembroke corgis owe much of their present popularity as pets to the fact that they are royal favourites.

Dogs helped Edward Elgar, the nineteenth century English composer, to become known. He had little success and was on the brink of despair when he finally won recognition with his Enigma Variations.

This music is made up of a set of sound descriptions of those nearest and dearest to him, and included his pet dogs. Nobody, before or since, has put dogs into a musical composition. But it was quite natural for Elgar to do so. The spaniels were his friends and part of his daily life. He took them along on his walks. He threw sticks into the river for them to retrieve. They loved to splash about in the water until they had found them. Then they would jump out and shake themselves vigorously. When you listen to the Enigma Variations it is easy to recognize the part which refers to his dogs.

Martin Niemoller, a Christian leader in Hitler's Germany, attracted worldwide admiration during the last war. He was not afraid to speak his mind against the Nazi regime, and quite soon found himself separated from his family and shut up in the notorious concentration camp at Dachau. When Germany was defeated and the brave man was released, he was treated as a hero and became a world figure. Niemoller received many letters of congratulation and a number of gifts from admirers. But no gift gave him more pleasure than that of Ratz, a dachshund. This little dog soon wormed his way into a very privileged position in his master's household. When Niemoller went to lecture in the United States, he carried a photo of his little dog in his wallet to remind him "that there is at least one creature in the world who will never breathe a word of criticism."

Ratz was allowed all sorts of liberties. When the pastor held conferences of local churchmen in his home, the dog sat on his own chair during the discussions. He usually behaved well, but there were occasional lapses. On his master's birthday he trailed a large ham around the guests in the dining room. On another occasion, he tore up a diploma which belonged to a learned visitor.

Niemoller eventually obtained another dog of the same breed, and named it Franz. Both dogs gave him enormous delight. He saw in them great qualities of loyalty which he knew most human beings did not possess.

Helen Keller, the amazing American woman, who had to struggle against blindness, deafness and dumbness, loved dogs. As a child her physical handicaps prevented her from communicating with her classmates. Only one managed to learn the finger language conveyed by touch of the deaf, dumb and blind. But all the children were kind to her.

One day, her classmates planned a surprise for her. Some

of the girls invited her to come and see "some jolly friends" they knew.

"That was all they would tell me," Helen Keller later wrote. "When we reached our destination they were very mysterious. I began to sniff and in a moment I realized that, instead of a human habitation we were entering a kennel, the abode of many Boston terriers. The dogs gave us a royal welcome, and one ugly beauty, heir of a noble pedigree, bestowed on me his special favour, placing himself resolutely at my feet and protesting with his whole body if I touched another dog. The girls asked me if I liked him. I said I adored him."

Helen's friend then told her to take it home. This was their gift to her. She learned that the dog's name was Sir Thomas of Belvedere.

"Sir Thomas seemed to understand; for he began spinning around and round like a top." But Helen decided to change his name to Phiz. "He assured me he had no objection to changing his name, and rolled over and over."

Phiz lived all his life with Helen Keller and she buried him at the end of a field under a white pine tree. "I grieved for him for a long time and resolved never to have another dog."

Yet another dog came into her life. Karsir was a three year old French bulldog, previously owned by a man. Karsir was suspicious of women. "He pondered over what we said to him and usually decided that it might be ignored. He did not want to lower himself by taking food from a woman and for a time refused his food.

"He found out quickly that apples could be used as a substitute for meat and bread. He learned to hold an apple in his paws and eat it with a good deal of gusto." The dog reached a compromise with his mistress in the end, but he always had a masculine swagger.

"There is not much to tell about Karsir—he found food abundant and obtainable with exertion; therefore he took advantage of every opportunity to gourmandize." Many dog owners will recognize their own pets in the French bulldog's attitude to life!

Another dog owned by Helen Keller was a brindle Dane, called Thora, who had eleven puppies: "I had not dreamed there would be so many, or that they would be so mischievous . . . They were as temperamental as poets and musicians are supposed to be. There was one singled out as the gem of the clan. We called her Siegliride and lavished special care and attention on her. She was red gold and her head was moulded on noble lines." Helen had a collie, Dusky, and Hans, another great Dane, at this time.

Because she had a spare barn, Helen Keller decided to enlarge her menagerie. She thought that many animals might like to live in it.

One day, while a friend was reading the advertisements in the *Boston Transcript* to her, tears came into her eyes when she heard of a woman who was going abroad and so could not take her Great Dane with her. Helen immediately offered it a home.

"I have never seen such a large dog," she wrote later. "He

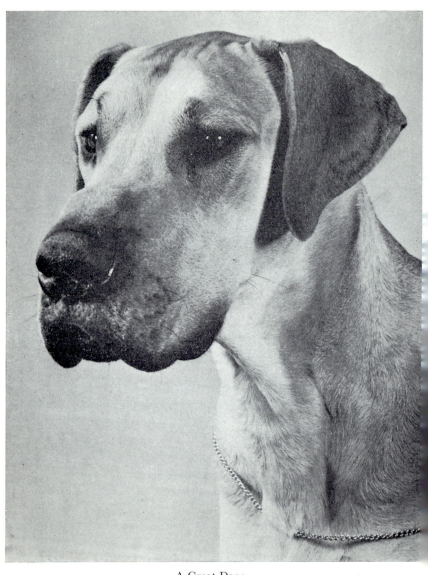

A Great Dane.

Photo: *Studio Lisa Ltd.*

was more like a young elephant then a dog." For Nimrod barged through the hall, knocking over a table lamp on his way. The crash seemed to upset him, for he ran into the dining room where he scattered the table laid for supper.

"Thora would have nothing to do with him. She even growled when he tried to make friends with her and her puppies. Out in the fields Nimrod seemed content to be by himself, but somebody noticed he was eating stones."

Later, the local veterinary decided that Nimrod's former owner had left some important facts out of the advertisement. The dog was about fourteen and had poor eyesight. He was eating the stones in the belief that they were bones!

Franklin D. Roosevelt, the former President of the United States, had a great love for animals, especially horses, ponies and dogs. There was nothing he enjoyed more than to escape from the worries of his work and go off riding with his wife and family, or take the dogs for a scamper.

His son, James, writes about the family's affection for dogs. "All of us were incorrigible dog lovers. There was usually a Scottie in the family, starting with the first, Duffy, bought in Scotland by Mother and Father on their honeymoon. A later Duffy was the family pet when father was stricken with polio in 1921, and mother today has acquired a Mr. Duffy. Fala, most famous of all father's Scotties is buried at Hyde Park, near the foot of father's grave. Another favourite pet, Chief, a police dog won by Anna in a raffle, is also buried in the rose garden." Hyde Park was the home of the Roosevelt family, which they preferred to the White House.

A Scottie looks at pictures.

Photo: *Studio Lisa Ltd.*

116

Roosevelt regarded his pets as friends. He gave them love and respect, which they returned. The year 1921 was the one in which he was stricken with poliomyelitis. Roosevelt had fallen overboard when sailing and had caught a slight chill. A few days later the chill was worse and he was advised to return home. When he left for New York, he had the Scottie, Duffy, cradled in his arms.

Fala, given to the President by a distant cousin, was his close companion during the war years. His name, Murray-the-Outlaw-of-Falahill, became well known to people all over the world. Fala was even subject of a great political controversy before the presidential election of 1944. Fala, the story went, had been left behind on the Aleutian Islands during an inspection of American installations. This had cost the American taxpayers many dollars for a destroyer had to be sent especially to pick up the Scottie. There was no truth in the tale, but the fact that it was believed at all showed how important the dog was supposed to be to the President.

Today, dogs live happier and longer lives than they did in the past. But, of course, conditions for them in the United States and Britain, and a few other dog-loving countries, are much more advanced than in many parts of the world.

And even in Great Britain there are still many unwanted dogs in the animals shelters. Some of them may have been genuinely lost, but most of them have been turned out by people who no longer care for them, who have found them a nuisance to look after, or do not want the expense of feeding them.

The A.S.P.C.A. alone has handled around 20,000 lost and abandoned dogs in a single year. However, there is still an overwhelming number of families who provide good homes for their pets.

Cruelty, unfortunately, is not yet a thing of the past. Sometimes a litter and bitch are abandoned, or a dog is left to starve, or is cruelly beaten. Happily these cases are not now as frequent as they were in the past.

Perhaps the most important change in the relationship between dogs and people is people's desire to own a dog for its own sake. They are kept for companionship, for their loyalty and because their owner likes a particular breed. It was once thought that when dogs were no longer used for the sports and hunting activities for which they had originally been bred, they would lose their particular characteristics. But this has not proved so. They have adapted well, just to becoming pets and companions. Some of their characteristics have even made a particular breed especially popular as a pet.

Most people are attracted to breeds which have gained fame in service, war, competitions, hunting and entertainment. Their very names are proof of the number of ways in which they have helped human beings. Dogs and people are bound together by many ties. Their future together should be just as fascinating as their past.

A Boston terrier with her puppies.
Photo: *Purina Pet Foods*

Index

Index

Index

Printed in England by C. Tinling & Co. Ltd.,
Liverpool, London and Prescot

DATE DUE

MAR 8			
	AP 10		
JAN 27	Staff		
FEB 04	Staff	OC 29 98	
MAY 2	OCT 7 '05		
MY 30 86			

636.7
Car

Carter, Richard Gordon

Dogs and people